GUARDRAILS:

How Free Minds Are Contained By False Narratives and

Conspiracy Rabbit Trails

Includes
GUARDRAILS
NIPSEY'S NOT DEAD
MANDOOZLED
WHY AUTOHOAXING MATTERS

By Tim Ozman
Copyright 2019

TABLE OF CONTENTS

INTRODUCTION

Guardrails starts with False Prophets, a short treatise explains how conspiracy theories are used to reinforce the big deceptions. It describes how free-thinkers are routinely brought back into the paddock. Many well-intentioned truthers have unwittingly helped to bury the very truth.

And just what is the truth buried by the conspiracy theories? Simple. The truth is, the media is not reporting factual events to inform you; they are reporting stories to conform you. And even if some see through it, there are ready-made conspiracy theories to explain away all the glitches in the matrix critical observers take note of.

Here is the shocking truth: conspiracy theories are part of the government-entertainment-media-complex. Those who are deconstructing the news and recognizing the psychological operations inherent in its dominant narratives are not conspiracy theorists. We're media analysts, critics, and deconstructionists.

The conspiracy theorists are the ones running around hunting the bad guy. Free-thinkers who can bypass political correctness and see through the propaganda don't need to insert hypothetical scapegoats into their assessment for a cohesive explanation. Nothing outside of logic is required to see the truth. The deception, on the other hand, requires several logical fallacies, most notably, an appeal to televised news as an authority.

In Part 2, The Metascript, I make the case for the existence of a hidden dictatorship governing the minds of all men through the manufacture of an artificial reality construct. The exemplar cited is the life and death of Nipsey Hussle, and how it relates to the fertility rites of mystery Babylon and the nightly news.

Part 3 Mandoozled contains the clearest and most definitive debunk of the Mandela Effect. Along with the deconstruction of the popular conspiracy theory is a cohesive explanation for why such a trick would be popularized in the days of real-time Autohoaxing. In Part 4, Guardrails closes with a strong case for shining a light on the real life consequences of psuedonews being imposed onto the consensus reality.

PART I
FALSE PROPHETS

ARE YOU STILL MEDIATED?

The media does its job so well people don't even seem to notice they're being mediated anymore. The media is the church of state. The religion is a secular world-spanning religion complete with eco-sins and eschatology in the form of ecological catastrophe to punish man for those eco-sins.

The hyper-mediated live in a worldview promulgated and reinforced by the media, infused with fake-news and pseudo-science. If you're not paranoid, you're not paying attention to the nightly news. It's a paranoia-inducing nightmare, which is why most people are either morbidly fascinated or utterly turned off.

Pseudonews is the concept, and the term"fake news" was meant to bury. Not anymore. Fake news doesn't encompass high-budget government productions known as Psychological Operations. If you think the pseudo in the news or the science is real, you are still mediated.

From a post-media perspective, the obvious problem is the fusion of fiction and news reporting. The public's trust in mediation has left it the exact state as believers in any religion, which offers explanations for the world events, a context within which it all makes sense. The priests are there to facilitate your mediation. t

THE PURPOSE OF CONSPIRACY THEORIES

"...follow the white rabbit."

Conspiracy theories generally refer to the alternative explanations for the alleged facts on the reported news. These are meant to entertain and tie up those minds who might otherwise see through the mediation itself.

Nearly every conspiracy theory exaggerates the power of the suspected conspirators to the point where they are now an elite, all-powerful cabal. They deepen the existing mediation. Instead of calling out the big lies, people are dragged into little clues of hidden truths deeper within.

This is analogous to people who aren't convinced of religion's claims and so seek deeper meaning but never quite finding evidence for their god, or their devil, outside of faith.

Notice how conspiracy theorists never meet Q's army of "white hats," nor are the blood-drinking bad guys ever exposed to the light?

CONSPIRACY THEORY or PSYOP FACT?

Psychological Operations are used to insert pseudonews events into the minds of the mediated as real events. The very existence of psyops is poorly understood today by most so-called "truthers."

Truthers who don't trust the official mainstream accounts of terrorist attacks or school shootings will gravitate toward

Every popular conspiracy theorist pushes "false flag" stories. I contend that these are there to conceal psychological operations. Here are a few things to take note of:

1. False flag theories are based on Operation Northwood, a proposed false flag operation against the Cuban government that originated within the U.S. Department of Defense (DoD).
2. This false explanation has been pushed by known shills like Alex Jones, Max Igan, and many others serving as Guardrails intentionally or not.

3. Even though false flags have never been proven, this conspiracy theory never ceases to be used as an explanation for psychological operations.

Psychological Operations, or psyops, make more sense for several reasons.

1. There is no reason to kill people during the production of perfectly legal propaganda for the nightly news. A death at a psyop would be as problematic as a death on a Hollywood movie set.
2. The special effects handle all the carnage you need.

Real death would be undesirable and unnecessary. It would turn a legal film production event into a war crime. The false flaggers insist these psuedonews events are real. As long as the events are assumed to be real, then the logical question is to ask, "who done it?"

Every scapegoat story is another diversion away from the truth. Psuedonews events are superimposed over reality. Much like indoctrination into false doctrines. The deceptions are reinforced by the neverending search for a villain. Meanwhile, the propaganda has done its work.

9/11 Truthers, who are still trying to blame someone other than Islam, are caught in this trap. They believe the scapegoat story about Osama Bin Laden is the wrong scapegoat. In the fight over scapegoats, an entire generation of truthers has chased the CIA's white rabbits, meanwhile wandering ever deeper into hyper-mediation.

False Flag explanations put one into a deeper state of mediation because these explanations proceed with an assumed reality to the events.

NO CRISIS ACTORS AT FALSE FLAG ATTACKS

If the event was real, then there would be no crisis actors. Why would actors perform on a set that explodes? Are crisis actors being killed? Obviously, that's not it. The mere presence of crisis actors implies that it is all scripted theatre. Also, if the event is real, then it implies a real attacker. There is automatically a scapegoat or a villain.

Psychological Operations do not require real attacks. Therefore, no real villains. This reveals the scapegoat as a psuedonews character existing only in the mediated reality and not in real life. This has huge implications for truthers who demonize Jews or for Democrats that demonize white kids with bowl cuts.

To accept a false flag theory is to accept a scapegoat. To accept a scapegoat story is to be among the mediated minds controlled by MSM drama.

Psychological operations do not require the reality of any of its villains.

What I am offering here is a post-media critique. Nobody has broken this down before because it's a fine point, and Autohoaxing wasn't this refined before.

False Flaggers are false prophets, and their premise is flawed on several key points. The fundamental misunderstanding spread by Bill Cooper and Bill Hicks alike.

Here are some key points:

1. A false flag is always thrown out there to misdirect the public.
2. false flag theories are a part of the psychological operation; they give it cover.
3. The presence of actors disproves false flag explanations. How many of these media events can you think of where there weren't actors?

Real people dying doesn't happen in the psyops because this would transform a perfectly legal propaganda film production event into a war crime packed with under-compensated potential whistleblowers.

This is the line the agents don't cross: you can't have False Flags AND Crisis Actors at the same scene.

False flags are never solved, yet hoaxes and Psyops are constantly exposed. This is the key. Ask your friendly neighborhood false flagger where they have seen a real false flag with a correctly identified scapegoat, where there weren't any actors or media foreknowledge.

The false flag narrative is spread by everyone but the autohoaxers. Non-autohoaxers are Guardrails for mainstream media narratives. They have to redirect free thinkers back into the box where they can be programmed to react to psuedonews events as though they were real.

If they don't have your attention, they can't instill fear.

False Flag Theory has hoodwinked the perceivers who otherwise would see past the rabbit trails and into the fake nature of it all.

The False Flag theories hide the psyops and reinforce the dominant paradigm. This alone accounts for the obvious pre-scripting and foreshadowing or false leads planted in full view of the public (as with Tom Hanks dropping suggestions that later would point to him as a suspect is Issac Kappy's fake death).

How many rappers do you see fake dying only to leave enigmatic clues before their death? As with the "Die Young" curse, named for Roddi Rich's track "Die Young," the prescription is evidence that it's all fake, and the rabbit trails placed there will reinforce the fake death because now it's a fake death with a mystery attached.

Could -predictive programming-- from the same media that provides the psyops, be a way to plant false leads and conspiracies in advance? This is not only plausible but observable. The same news outlets who bring you the nightly psyop are providing eerie hints of foreknowledge. This is just good filmmaking. Foreshadowing is a good literary technique.

The themes in entertainment tend to match those in the psyops. This is intentional. It heightens suggestibility to the storylines in the news. The psyops are scripted to reinforce existing tensions and dialectics.

With regards to 11-3, I suspect now that we're not supposed to spot the signs until after. When that one steadily went viral, there were many false flag proponents all of a sudden warning people of an incoming "false flag."

This is possibly due to habit. Or perhaps it's because nobody has offered a better term to use. So from this point on, anyone pushing false flag should be required to show us where one happened, who did it, and was it bereft of crisis actors or media foreshadowing?

For a list of exposed hoaxes, consult Autohoax.com. For a list of False Flags, choose your favorite unsolved conspiracy theory.

PREDICTIVE SCRIPTING PROVES REALITY METASCRIPTING

Mass media foreshadowing events isn't the result of coincidence. There are no coincidences in a script. The psuedonews events directing the lives of the masses are scripted and presented as real by the same screens projecting the entertainment media. These are reinforced by celebrities who bridge the gap between entertainment (which itself is immersion in pseudo-reality) and psuedonews.

Mass media foreshadowing gives away the basic fact that there is a bigger story under which the rest operate. This bigger story is the metascript.

The metascript is an artificial reality construct. When observing instances of foreshadowing or predictive programming, the following options are apparent:

1. Possible false flag attack
2. A possible attack which is not a false flag
3. Possible psychological operation

There has never been an event predicated or mirrored in the entertainment media, which manifests as an actual "false flag."

However, there are many psyops foreshadowed, or otherwise hinted at in the mass media. This would include instances of faked celebrity deaths attended by mysterious and enigmatic conspiracy theories.

I think they use conspiracy theorists agents to chant "false flag" as an alternative to the mainstream reports. This is not truth-telling; it's alternative media narratives that function as Guardrails.

Chanting "false flag!" or "inside job" is still saying, "we're under attack!"

False flag explanations, never proven to be true, are also used to make people side against people instead of recognizing that the mediated worldview is a construct not worth fighting over. False flag narratives keep people inside the artificial reality construct where all those atrocious psuedonews events are real.

In the movie The Village, monsters prowl the perimeter of the peaceful community and prevent anyone from leaving. Later it is discovered that the monsters are the elders in disguise. Outside, the village was a saner world unconfined by superstitious dread and baseless fears. False flag theories to adds an additional level of fear to the terror theatre. Now, the already scary news is worse. This tends to frighten most back into the village, the mainstream worldview.

Those who see through the disguises and the psyops can't be terrorized because they know it's "only a movie."

ALL PRE-SCRIPTED PSUDEO-NEWS EVENTS OCCUR WITHIN A METASCRIPT

The metascript is the story within which all the other stories take place, the place where entertainment fiction and psuedonews fiction merge. This would include the eschatological script inherent in the climate change narrative, a secular doomsday. Those who believe we're following a path to civilizational destruction in ten years because of our eco-sins are following a metascript.

The Bible is another metascript. So is the Koran. There are competing worldviews, and the dominant ones today are fighting over the interpretation of reality. This interpretation, this official worldview, is the religion used to conform and control the masses.

The mainstream mediated world view is the state church today. It is the new living bible. They write it as they go, but it follows the bit story and remains within those parameters. It's no different than a highly curated holy book. Its authority is just as suspect.

The mass media is telling Myths. Against the backdrop of real news, real culture, and real happenings, they have their metastory, which is nothing more than a pre-scripted history that the day to day happenings are conformed to.

Pre-scripting in the entertainment media foreshadowing future psyops happens anyway. What part of nightly propaganda isn't setting the stage for future scenes? There is mainstream pre-scripting and foreshadowing for uncritical thinkers, and there are alternative explanations and rabbit trails for those who look closer.

The metascript contains scripts which create rabbit holes to intentionally lead people to false flag conclusions, rather than calling it all pre-scripted.

Ultimately the false flag conclusion hides the psyop behind narratives that are inside of and dependent upon the metascript. For example, debating how man causes much global warming assumes one accepts the metascript of global warming itself. If one rejects that, then debating the degree of change is outside of reality.

Leaving the mediated worldview behind means leaving behind its monsters and its doomsdays. Many people leave their religions behind and with it, those false explanations and those baseless fears and misplaced hopes. Leaving the dominant religion today, the hypermediated worldview which enchants the masses is an essential step towards restoring free will.

So long as you're in their artificial reality construct, you're subject to its fears.

Many, if not all, psyops are preceded by Media references, which give false leads about the incoming event. False flag is just a new term for scapegoating, and when you control the scapegoat, you can prevent it from ever getting caught.

The "truth" movements like 9-11 Truth uses the metascripts when forming their conspiracy explanations, all of which are labeled as false flags while disagreeing on the appropriate scapegoat. The 9-11 truthers don't disagree with the media on the essentials of what happened. They just think it was worse.

By making the "truth" about the news way scarier, it becomes less attractive, and it goes against the average person's cognitive bias towards easier or less emotionally unsettling explanations. In this way, conspiracy theories Guardrail the mainstream news. They've been doing this since JFK's alleged assassination. This is formulaic. The false flag conspiracy theories all operate within the mainstream metascript.

The scripting and predictive programming come from the same source as the mainstream foreshadowing. It proves that all media is centralized and has a central directorship. There is no meaningful distinction to be made between news media and entertainment media.

Planted hints of media foreknowledge demonstrate that the psychological operations are written into the metascript and that the foreshadowing isn't predictive as much as it's preparatory.

Entertainment and news reporting follows the same Metascript. Conspiracy theories with false flags and scapegoats do the same.

POST MEDIA

Autohoaxers are the only ones who get it right. The World Stage is real. The artificial reality construct and its metascripts are now laid bare for anyone to see. It is the de facto state-church: you're not at home watching Netflix.; you're at church. You're not in science class learning about reducing carbon dioxide; you're at church learning about reducing sin; you're not only getting higher education; you're also being surreptitiously indoctrinated at the church of state.

What do we do with this? The answer is simple. Rather than fear the Wizards of Oz, we need to see past the special effects and movie magic. The more of us who call it out, the greater the possible apostasy.

Right now, fake trumps real because the mediated minds comprise most of the population. That can change. Religions come and go; maybe it's time this one does too.

FALSE PROPHETS

False flaggers are false prophets. Their premise is flawed on several key points. This is largely a matter of mis-education and it can be repaired.

Conspiracy theorists who start with the assumption that every terror attack is a "false flag" aren't unveiling "truths". They are obscuring it and redirecting free-thinking minds back to the mainstream. These theorists serve as Guardrails.

The purpose of "predictive programming" is both narrative preparation for future psuedonews and cover for psychological operations. This shows the collusion between the entertainment industry and the news media, another fact which debunks the assertions of conspiracy theorists chasing scapegoat stories when the storyteller itself is not to be trusted.

The Guardrails allow the news media to get away with fabricating events for propaganda purposes. In this sense, the false flaggers and the mainstream media are on the same team.

PART 2

THE METASCRIPT

An example from real life.

THE METASCRIPT

THE WORLD
STAGE HAS A
"METASCRIPT"

There's a Metascript framing world events. There is evidence of reality tampering. not in the mystical *"Mandela Effect"* sort of way, but more in a way that humanity is being guided by stories.

Fake news is just the tip of the iceberg. The agit-prop serves a deeper purpose than steering votes. The dramatic events we see on the news are often discovered to be psychologically impactful propaganda films presented as real, at least to those that dig deeper.

The new world order already exists. It preexisted all the conspiracy theories about the new world order. It's already been here and right now they're just reconfiguring it for the new age.

People have been seeing the puzzle pieces for years, but now are putting them together in new ways.

Here we're looking at a pattern, a discernible pattern. Many scripts are being played out right in front of us. The staged life and death of Nipsey Hussle and this is just one example.

Another example of how pervasive this scripting goes, note how the wrath of globe has replaced the wrath of God for the atheist. The believers are in an end-times frame of mind. Yet, the climate change end-times scenario is another script. The world is not changing because of man.

This Metascript is a story imposed onto reality.

THE MARATHON AS ALLEGORY

The world stage is the faked version of reality that the public accepts as real. The mainstream media is the de facto state religion. The MSM worldview is presented to you as daily news events, all of which are believed by the mediated masses to be "real life" events.

The enigmatic death of Nipsey Hussle and the events surrounding it gives away a lot about the big program. There's a framework within which these scripted events are occurring and it has to do with the sun, the seasons, and what the sun gods are said to be doing at each stage of the year from solstice to solstice, equinox to equinox.

So let's start with this. The marathon begins.

- The Marathon was released on the 2010 winter solstice. This is the traditional birthdate for the sun god and his starting point.

- The Marathon Store opened on the summer Solstice of 2017.

Nipsey Hussle OPENS "The Marathon Store" at the **GRAND OPENING** in **Los Angeles, CALIFORNIA** off of **Slauson & Crenshaw** at 3420 W. Slauson Ave.

Nipsey cutting the Ribbon to his **GRAND OPENING** of #TheMarathon Store

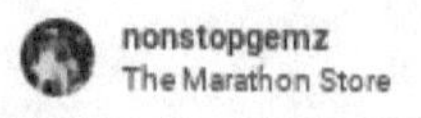

nonstopgemz
The Marathon Store

View Profile

- Nipsey's death was on the astronomical Easter, not the one the public celebrates.

- His posthumous humanitarian award was awarded on the summer solstice of 2019

-

- The announcement of the planned Nipsey Hussle Memorial Tower was made in August, his birth month.

- A gate was erected at The Marathon, signifying the Lion's Gate. **"Lion's Gate** is a cosmic **alignment** that opens every year on August 8th to the 12th, when the Sun is in Leo and is marked by the **star Sirius** and it's closer relationship to Earth while **aligning** in Orion's belt, which perfectly syncs up with the Pyramids in Giza."

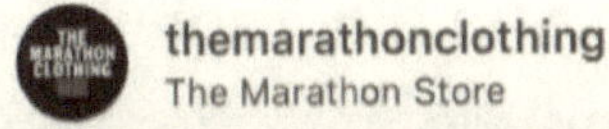

themarathonclothing
The Marathon Store

· · ·

THE MARATHON CLOTHING

As a notice to the public, we're putting up a gate on Thursday, August 1st, 2019 to enclose the plaza at 3420 W. Slauson Ave to start the early development stages of the forthcoming Nipsey Hussle Tower to commeroate and honor the life and legacy of Nipsey. The Marathon Store will remain closed, but you can shop online at TheMarathonClothing.com

Thank you,
The Marathon Clothing

themarathonclothing #NipseyHussleTower

- "The Marathon Don't Stop," a biography of Nipsey Hussle will be released on the astronomical Easter which falls on March 24, 2020.

BET

A Nipsey Hussle Biography 'The Marathon Don't Stop' Is Coming Out Soon

Nipsey Hussle's story is already a part of hip-hop's history, but now it will be immortalized in a biography. According to Complex, VIBE ...

2 weeks ago

OCCULT RITUALS IN PUBLIC

What I'm describing here is an occult ritual performed in public over a period of time. It is a timeless script played out according to the solar calendar and its festivals at the major quadrants of the year.

The Marathon is a scripted storyline based upon a modern christ figure or sun personification.

It describes the journey of the sun from birth to death to rebirth as it cycles above and it represents, of course, the life cycles from birth to death as it goes from winter solstice where it is born to its annual death.

The marathon is a metaphor for the sun's never-ending journey.

Nipsey Hussle exits the world stage on March 31st, 2019 when he is murdered.

This is the astronomical Easter and Nipsey was 33. So this is where you get the initial archetype of Christ who died at 33.

Upon examining his death, there are several things immediately connecting him to the story of Christ. Initial descriptions of him by witnesses on the scene painted a picture. This picture led people to speculate on who did it and why.

Here are a few early characterizations:
- He was "assassinated" as it was described by LAPD just before he was supposed to meet with them and discuss ways to bring peace between the Bloods and Crips. This shows Nipsey to be a bringer of peace.

- In a Tweet he sent just 90 minutes before he was gunned down, Hussle wrote: "Having strong enemies is a blessing." A Christ-like message of loving one's enemies.

  Having strong enemies is a blessing.

  3:52 PM · Mar 31, 2019 · Twitter for iPhone

  182.5K Retweets   **339.4K** Likes

- It was speculated his upcoming documentary about Dr. Sebi would have made him a target. Sebi is alleged to have cured blindness, AIDS, leprosy, and other ailments, making him a healer and a hero to those who believe his cures are being suppressed. It's very Christ-like to be a healer outside of "Big Pharma".

- He was characterized as Jesus Christ in the flesh by his closest friends in statements immediately after his death. The iconography of his pre-death GQ photoshoot is loaded with symbolism alluding to his upcoming role as a sacrificial sun king.

The death was reported by TMZ and it had all the trappings of a staged, simulated death along with the enigmatic occult overtones. TMZ sounded out is phonetically similar to TAMMUZ, the Babylonian sun God also born on the winter solstice.

Tammuz the Shepherd

This is more than just a reference that comes up again and again. It's a Babylonian reference worth noting here. The immediate characterizations of the rapper painted him up as a Christ-like character, including his childhood friend and fellow rapper daylight who said Nipsey was literally Jesus Christ.

L.A rapper Daylyt Says Nipsey Hussle was Jesus Christ ...
https://www.youtube.com › watch
Apr 6, 2019 - Uploaded by Young Moses
L.A rapper **Daylyt** believes **Nipsey** Hussle was **Jesus Christ** #NipseyHussle #
JesusChrist #Daylyt.

Daylyt Believes Nipsey Hussle Was Jesus Christ ... - YouTube
https://www.youtube.com › watch
Apr 6, 2019 - Uploaded by KollegeKidd.com
Subscribe: https://www.youtube.com/channel/UCXpGi22cKtuNtiKUqFjj8BQ?
sub_confirmation=1 ~Follow https ...

NIPSEY HUSSLE (WAS JESUS CHRIST REINCARNATED ...
https://www.youtube.com › watch
Apr 13, 2019 - Uploaded by SCOOP TV
NIPSEY HUSSLE (WAS **JESUS CHRIST** REINCARNATED, SAYS **DAYLYT**)(
APR 2019). SCOOP TV ...

According to the reports, he was about to meet the
chief of police in Los Angeles to discuss bringing peace
between the Crips and the Bloods. Rumors circulated at

his death at that scene that this was done to stop him from publicizing the work of dr Sebi who was said to be able to cure AIDS, blindness, cancer, leprosy.

He was described as "a god" at his death scene by the crisis actors. They said he was a god, he wasn't a regular person. They kept calling him a God.

He was also described as this benefactor to the poor. As an entrepreneur, you can see him in videos helping the poor, handing out money, handing out clothes and weed to the poor.

This was all part of characterizing him as a Christ, passing out the loaves, the fish, curing leprosy, curing the blind, bringing peace, all very Christ-like dying at 33 as he walked to the spot where he was going to be killed between two other gangsters, he was carrying his son, who happens to be named Kross.

FORESHADOWING AS EVIDENCE OF SCRIPTING

His death was foreshadowed in his lyrics and videos and the GQ photoshoot right before his Easter death on March 31st, 2019. The LAPD was insinuated to be assassins in a Simpson's poster included in that shoot. Note the police chief's gun and how it's pointing at Nipsey. There is also a man on the roof behind the police chief and Lauren is looking like she's in the know.

This is noteworthy considering the initial conspiracy theories speculated that the LAPD was involved, as they were supposed to meet with Nipsey over ending gang violence the very next day.

Nipsey Hussle's planned meeting with L.A. police on gang ...
https://www.nbcnews.com › news › us-news › nipsey-hussle-s-planned-me... ▾
Apr 1, 2019 - A **meeting** requested by slain rapper **Nipsey** Hussle with Jay-Z's Roc Nation entertainment company and officials from the **Los Angeles Police Department** on combating gang violence will still take place. Los Angeles **Police** Commissioner Steve Soboroff told NBC News on Monday that ...

Nipsey Hussle Was Hailed as a Peacemaker by the LAPD. He ...
https://www.nytimes.com › 2019/07/15 › nipsey-hussle-investigation
Jul 15, 2019 - LOS ANGELES — The memory of the rapper **Nipsey** Hussle still looms ... The head of the **police** commission said he had plans to **meet** with ...

Nipsey Hussle Was Going To Meet With LAPD To Discuss ...
https://www.billboard.com › articles › columns › hip-hop › nipsey-hussle-... ▾
Apr 1, 2019 - **Nipsey** Hussle was murdered less than a day before the Compton rapper was slated to **meet** with the **LAPD** to discuss ways to stop gang ...

Roddi Rich's song "Die Young" features Nipsey Hussle in the video at 1:33 and the video is filmed in a cemetery. The lyrics foretell Nipsey's death. The song is produced by "London on da track" and Roddie Rich performed it live on March 13th, in London (3/31).

Roddy Rich Predicted Nipsey Death 2

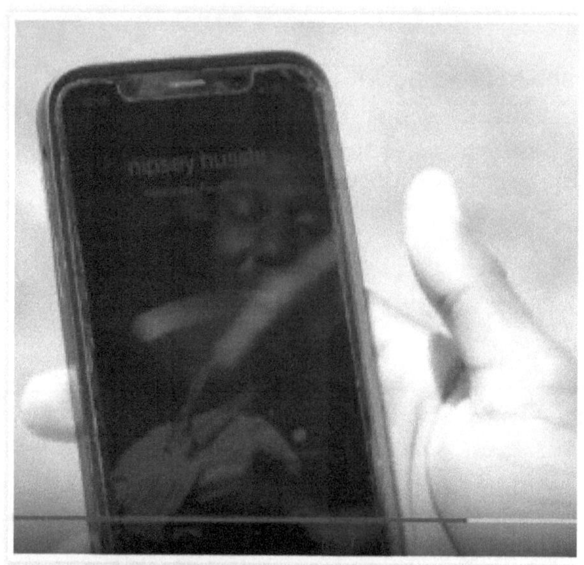

133 is symbolic of one, it's the Psalm used during Masonic ritual (during which initiates are symbolically killed and resurrected), and two, in its reversal, it's his death date, 3/31.

A so-called "Die Young curse" has afflicted more than Nipsey Hussle and is highly suggestive of a whole lot of scripted events passed off as entertainment and celebrity news. This isn't unlike other celebrity death curses, such as the "27 club" which took the life of Jim Morrison, who was widely reported as having a Jesus Christ Complex.

FUNERARY RITES

Sun's "Funeral Procession" ends with its death, then rebirth.

Jesus' death and rebirth follows the Sun's annual trek, or lap, aka, the MARATHON.

The death and funeral of Nipsey Hussle was part of the mass public ritual. He was reenacting the sun god killed at 33. He takes on the role of the sun and his "Marathon" is the sun's journey.

His funeral procession was the length of a standard marathon. During the funeral rites Lauren London, his spouse, plays the role of the goddess Isis in a state of mourning.

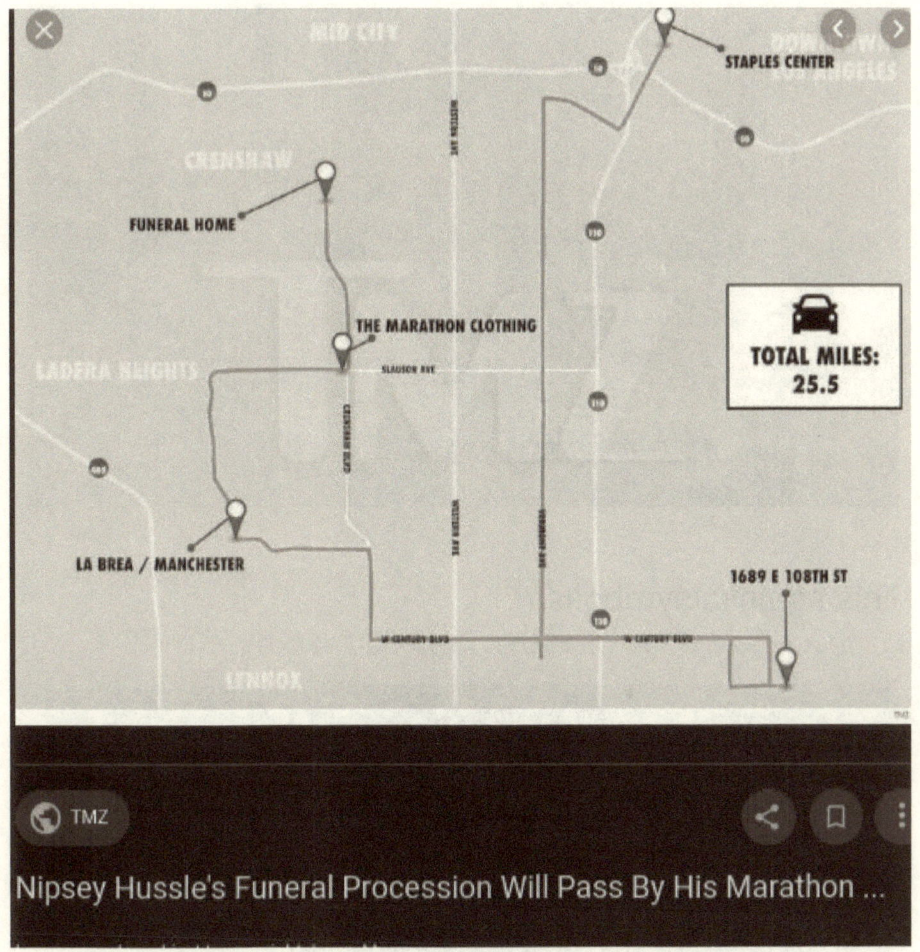

Nipsey Hussle's Funeral Procession Will Pass By His Marathon ...

During the marathon, Lauren was throwing cash out the windows of the hearse.

This again is symbolism.

Money tossed out window of Nipsey Hussle funeral motorcade vehicles I ABC7

They were on a marathon-length funeral procession and Lauren playing the goddess Isis/ Virgo/ Ishtar/etc was throwing money in the street, and obvious and interesting reference to the upcoming London marathon sponsored by Virgin Money.

ISIS AND OSIRIS

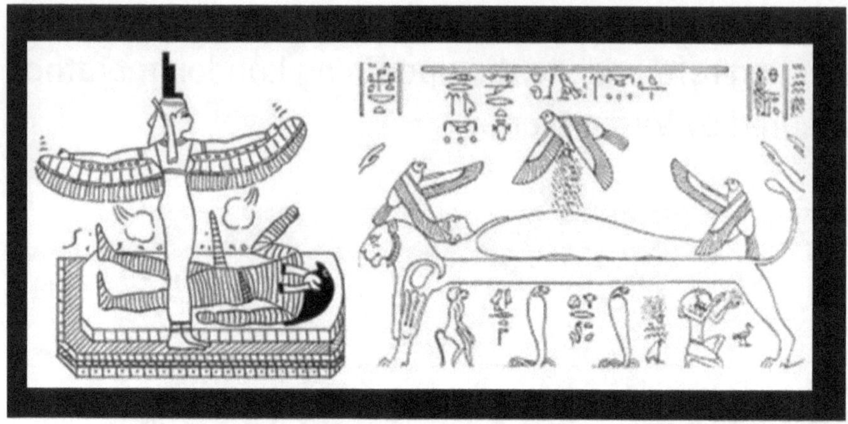

However the particular myth is played out, Osiris is killed and he's dismembered. His phallus is chopped off and his dead body is scattered across the darkness. The next part of the myth is about a widow who's in mourning. Nipsey and Lauren identified themselves as ISIS and Osiris in a photoshoot preceding his staged murder.

The subtext within the script is what stands out here. The deeper meanings which only make sense with the Metascript in mind. The names, dates, numbers, and correlate to where the sun is. This is an iteration of Mystery Babylon, the Roman Sun cult, which has more ancient origins.

During the procession, Nipsey's mother said, "our engine is on fire burning but not destroyed."

This figures into the Metascript during the following Holy Week celebrations when Notre Dame cathedral burned.

"Our Lady" is another goddess reference and she was burning.

This was foreshadowed by the line "our engine is on fire, burning but not destroyed," spoken as the mother of the Christ in this story. Her demeanor was remarked upon for its strangeness and lack of grief. She made the peculiar suggestion that we pray to Nipsey as he was freer to do his life's work without his body.

The ritual dismemberment represents the sun god losing the battle against the night. Before the sun can come back and defeat the night, he has to be reborn. His dismemberment at the hands of the god of death is played out often in films, movies, and literature. In Star Wars, the scene where Darth Vader chops off Luke Skywalker's hand is consistent with the Astrotheological mythos.

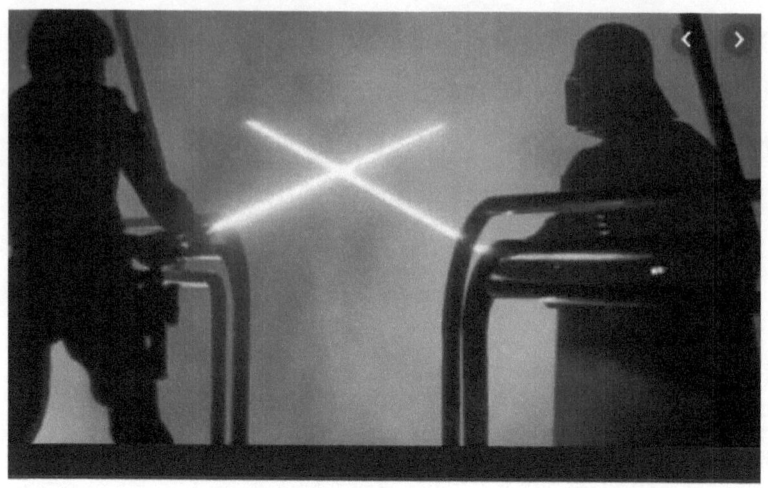

In this case, the severing of the sword hand represents the loss of his life-giving power and the victory of death over life. The severed phallus is lost for good. This is why ISIS plants the obelisk in its place over his buried body.

Luke Skywalker falls and hangs in Cloud City before he's rescued and they reattach his sword hand. This is a symbolic story that's constantly being retold.

It occurs again with Luke hanging, having lost his sword:

This time the "force" brings it with his grasp and he liberates himself from the beast. This is the universal myth being retold to every demographic. It's an ancient story reborn here with the character Nipsey Hussle playing Christ. His dismemberment and remembrance will be described in the following chapters.

THE STEEPLE FALLS

The entire story is spread out over time and it's told symbolically. For instance, he's carrying his son named Kross to the place where he was murdered. The images of his son show a child dressed like his father, even down to the hairstyle. This is symbolic of the sun god reincarnating as himself.

Kross Asghedom Bio, Age, Parents ...
informationcradle.com

The part where the sun god is castrated plays out when Notre Dame burned. Sunset is when the sun god dies. The god of darkness, Seth, or Set, defeats the sun god at the "setting" of the sun.

The steeple is just an obelisk representing the same sun god and this same eternal myth. It's encoded into the Christian churches to this day, even the non-Catholic denominations. The atheists worship the obelisk in its modern form, the rocket, and the statists worship it in the form of Washington Monument. This cult has many faces. It gives itself away in the pageantry and theatre.

The steeple fell at sunset. Supposedly the crown of thorns worn by Jesus Christ himself was nearly engulfed in the flames.

This is all evidence of Metascripting. It connects the entertainment news, celebrity news, the news media, and the political news. This ties it all together. It certainly has a central director. The prefabricated news and the general narratives were exposed throughout this operation.

During the time that the crown of thorns of Christ is being rescued from the burning cathedral and the steeple was falling, Nipsey Hussle is being presented all over social media wearing a crown of thorns.

He also made an appearance in My Pet Goat 2, in which a Christ figure is watching something burn as a steeple on a cathedral falls behind him.

1280 × 720
YouTube
Notre Dame Cathedral Spire collapse in I PET GOAT II

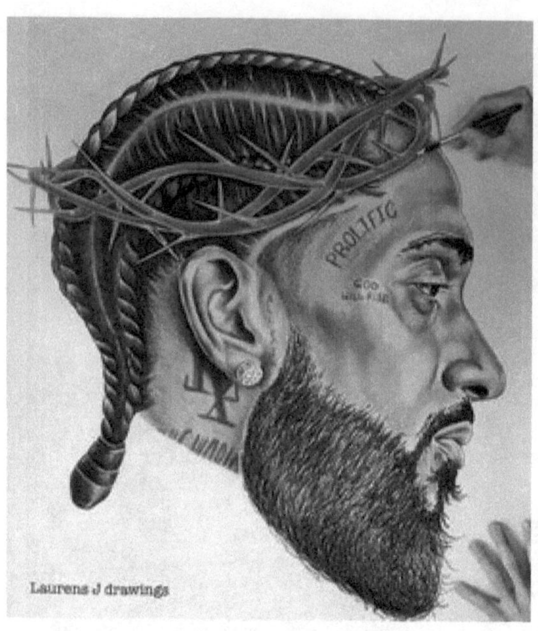

Again, these are not coincidences. These are overlapping, interrelated storylines. Later, in August of 2019, the Nipsey Hussle Memorial Tower is announced to be erected at the place of his death, which happens to be on the 33rd parallel.

But back to Holy Week:

The International Space Station plays a role in the story.

This is another goddess reference. The goddess of the night sky, ISIS is presented to secular society as the

ISS. There are many astrotheological references in the space opera believed by many to be a space program.

We have our scripted reality, below and above.

From above, the astronauts in the space station said they could see the three bee habitats on the roof had survived the fire.

Here's where you get into Masonic history. This is some deep scripting with layers of subtext.

"Our engine is on fire, burning but not destroyed," is a reference to the Phoenix, a mythical creature that sets itself on fire only to be reborn. This is a symbol that is prevalent throughout the scripted world stage dramas.

In the context of the lifecycle of the sun god, the death and rebirth. The sun god is the phoenix and therefore the "burning man".

HI K.J... FYI, PENIS IS AN OCCULT ABBREVIATION OF PHOENIX. I am an etymologist.
I enjoy your work. Thanks, Dezert.

The ISS is a temple for the modern high priesthood. It's a cathedral up in Heaven and from up there they can see that although Our Lady may have burned, she'll be back. They report the "god's eye view".

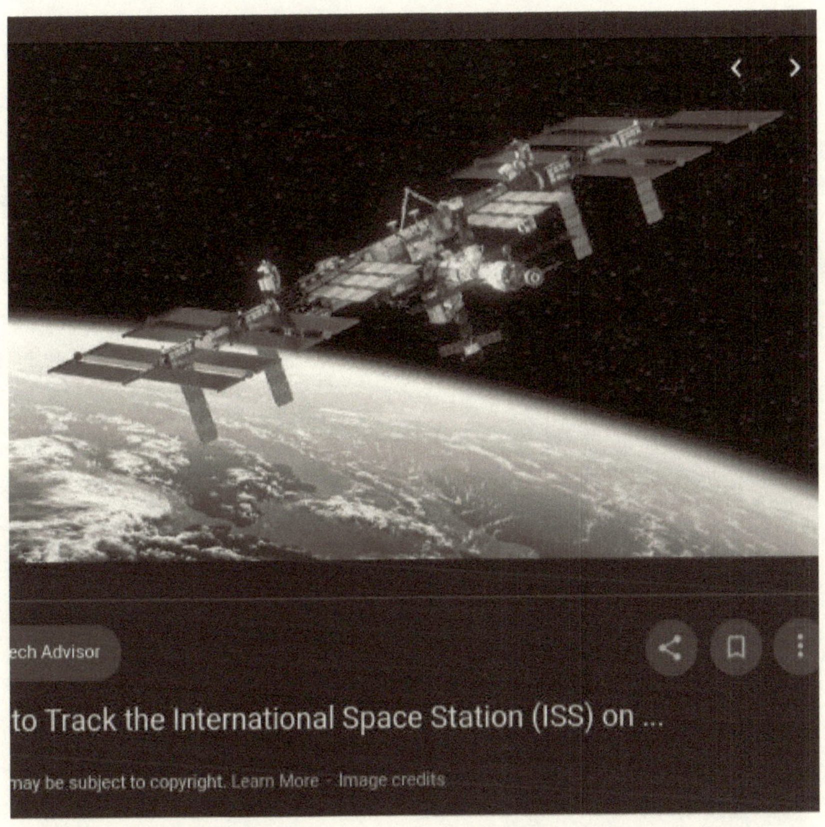

The astronauts reported seeing three beehives structures on the roof. The symbol of the hexagon is inherent in the beehive. This is also referencing the "Rolling sixties" as well as the hexagram, comprised of three 60 degree angles.

This Satanic symbol has nothing to do with King David, the greatest king of Israel. It is the Satanic Hexagram from which we get the word 'Hex' ie. to curse or cast a spell !

end

The three beehives on the roof of the cathedral that survived the fire each had 60,000 bees.
The Beehive is a symbol of the Knights Templar.

This was said to be a miracle.

In reality, it was scripted as was the fire. A man in Knights Templar armor was spotted on the tower.

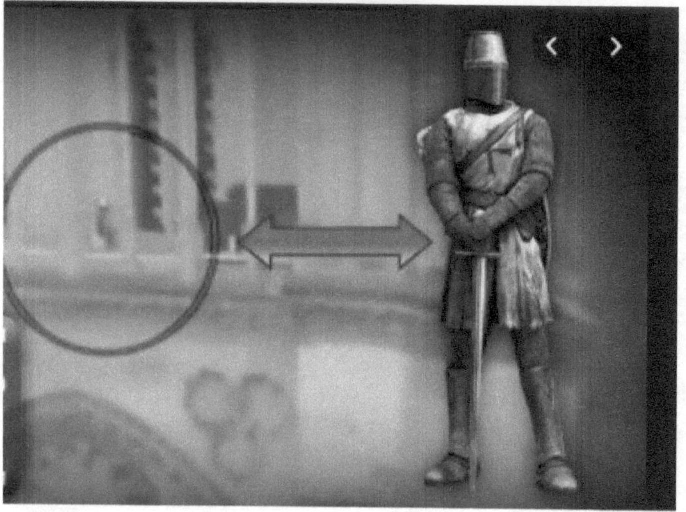

This is consistent with the story of the cathedral's financiers, the Templars who were burned at the stake, but they survived by going underground and they re-emerged as the Freemasons in 1717

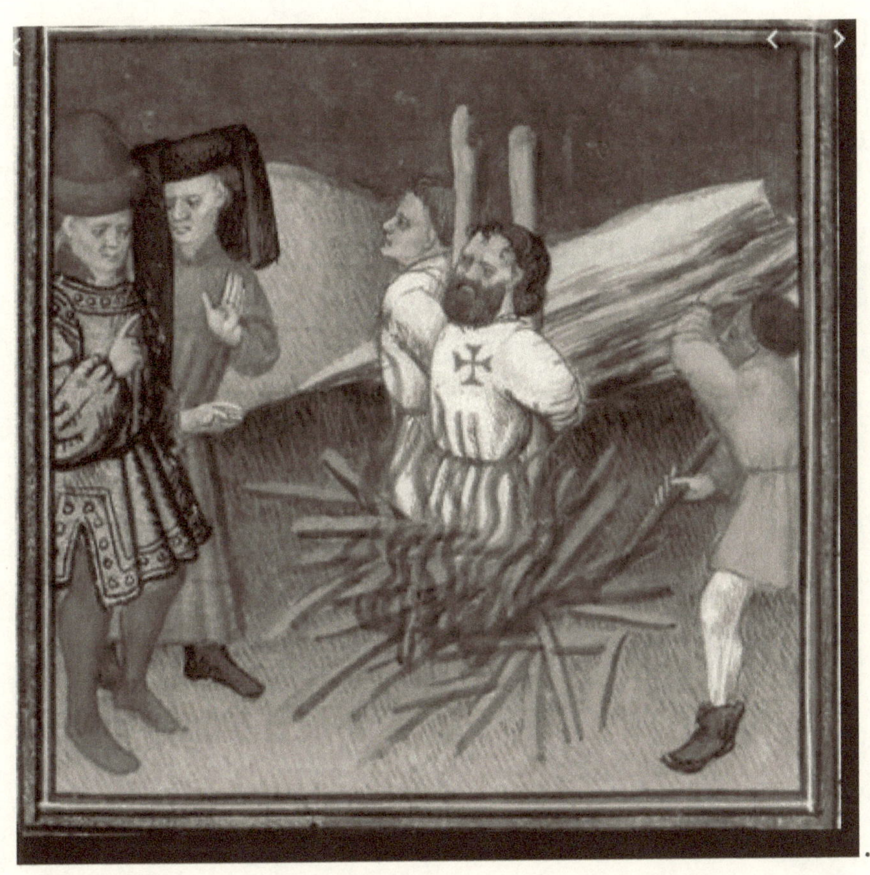

Burned but not destroyed. Very phoenix-like. The Knights Templar were burned at the stake and went underground. So here you've got the beehive symbol of the temple.

A Templar Knight in the burning cathedral--that's burning but not destroyed according to the space station and the mother of the character playing Christ.

ISIS, the mother saying, you know, we're not destroyed because of course, it's a show of faith. We know he's going to be reborn. The marathon will continue.

PHOENIX FROM THE FLAMES

There was a 33-year-old man who burned in front of the White House. Like the death of Nipsey Hussle, this was released through TMZ. He was wearing a shirt that had USA in large letters on the front.

This Babylon burning symbolism. Babylon is another name of the goddess ISIS/ Virgo. This archetype relates to the burning cathedral, Our Lady burning. So this guy's burning himself in front of the White House with a USA shirt and they show the obelisk behind him.

Who set themselves on fire in front of the White House?

WASHINGTON — A man who **set himself on fire** Wednesday in a park south of the **White House** has died, the United States Park Police said early Thursday. The man was identified as Arnav Gupta, 33, of Bethesda, Md. He had been reported missing by the Montgomery County Police Department on Wednesday. May 30, 2019

Man Who Set Himself on Fire Near the White House Dies From Injuries

https://www.nytimes.com › politics › arnav-gupta-man-on-fire-dies

TMZ makes sure to get the Washington Memorial obelisk in the shot. This illustrates the connection between the burning man and the symbol of resurrection. This is dramatized annually at the Washington MEmorial at the Catharsis:

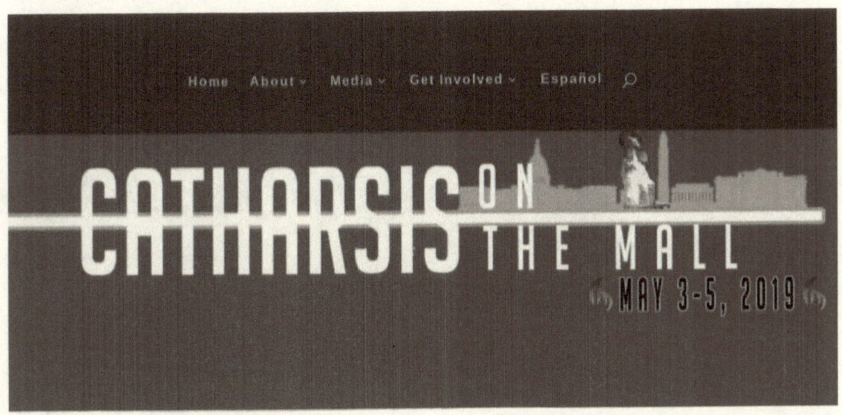

Now, the odd thing is it was 33 years since the last time someone burned themselves to death in front of the White House.

Man Lights Self Afire Outside White House in Protest

JAMES ROWLEY   February 15, 1986

Click to copy

WASHINGTON (AP) _ An unemployed man lit his gasoline-soaked body on fire outside the White House after writing to President Reagan complaining about the economy and the nation's veterans programs, officials said Saturday.

So think about it: the last time was 33 years ago. Was he was reborn to do it again in 33 years? The scripting here is obvious. There's even more to this because this is also the 33rd year of the Burning Man festival. That also started 33 years ago.

Burning Man gathering in Nevada desert poses challenges ...
https://www.naco.org › articles › burning-man-gathering-nevada-desert-po... ▾
Aug 19, 2019 - **Burning Man** will draw thousands of revelers to the Northwest Nevada ... 25 for
Burning Man, the **33rd year** of a gathering that involves the ...

This seemed to predict the death at the Burning Man festival this year: a 33-year-old died under mysterious circumstances.

Search instead for 33 year old dies at burning mn

Burning Man death: What we know about the man who died at ...
https://www.usatoday.com › story › entertainment › celebrities › 2019/08/30 ▾
Aug 30, 2019 - A **33-year-old** man **died** Thursday at **Burning Man** in the Black Rock Desert north
of Reno, Nevada. His **death** is being investigated as ...

It should also be pointed out that it's been 33 years since the Challenger explosion.

Also worth noting: the Dark Phoenix movie posters were out and depicted a space shuttle in flames. Again, foreshadowing.

THIS MOVIE DEBUTED AT 33 MILLION DOLLARS, and is 113 minutes long*

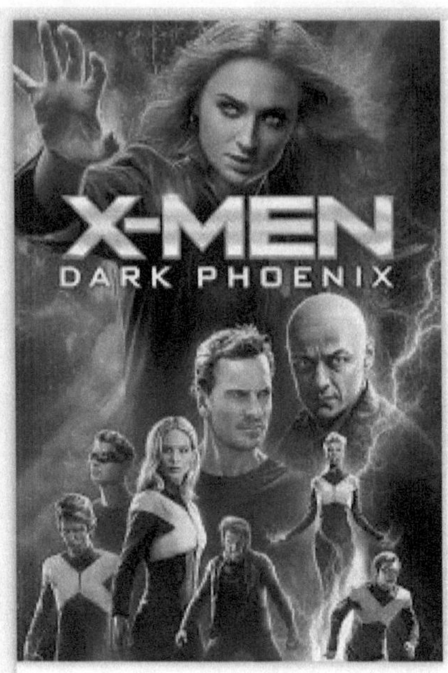

Dark Phoenix

June 2019   113 minutes
Action & adventure

Add to Wishlist

There was further evidence of scripting on the summer solstice, tying into this story of the sun's journey/marathon. On that day the city of Phoenix, on the 33rd parallel, was burning and was partially evacuated.

Woodbury Fire hits 66,000 acres; community meeting Friday ...
https://www.azcentral.com › news › local › arizona-wildfires › 2019/06/21 ▾
Jun 21, 2019 - Woodbury **Fire** hits 66,000 acres; community meeting set for **Friday** evening ...... Woodbury wildfire back burn at Roosevelt Lake, **June 21**, 2019.

It was reported that there was a Phoenix seen in the Aurora Borealis as observed from a Russian military base.

And if that's not enough, after 33 years of being in a vault, an unreleased track by Freddy Mercury surfaced just as the planet Mercury revealed itself alongside the summer solstice sun, this being significant because mercury is the God of marathons. This track "Time waits for no one" is thematically connected to the Metascripting, and it ties in to the astrotheological narrative, in which the planet makes an appearance alongside the sun. Freddie Mercury and Nipsey Hussle, Sun and Mercury.

Nipsey store, the marathon Mercury's the God of thieves. Merchants.Additionally, the symbol of the eternal flame, the torch being passed, is inherent in this story.

Many of us had predicted a bombing at the end of the London marathon. And the reason why we said this was there was a conspicuous "cowboy" character at Nipsey's death scene who seemed to be similar or analogous to the cowboy character at the Boston bombing marathon.

All the talks about the marathon and this cowboy character seemed to presage a terror attack at a public event.

The Metascript was bringing up the specter of ISIS. So we predicted that ISIS would strike at the end of the London marathon. That was our prediction. And ISIS did attack. They bombed churches on Easter. Easter is about the sun god's funeral rites. Jesus, a 33 year old, is draped in purple during this time, a color associated with the Phoeicians, and therefore the Phoenix.

Holy week was hit with a bombing at the end of the sun god's procession. The symbolic processions at the churches celebrating Easter were hit. But the London Marathon's "Virgin Money" procession was not. It was a mirror of Nipsey's funeral procession with Lauren London throwing money out the window. This symbolically merged the marathon with procession, Nipsey and Christ, and the Easter bombings with with the predictive scripting of the "Cowboy" at The Marathon's "finish line", which is the sun god's death scene.

So I think it was scripted in there pretty well. They preemptively censored the internet in Sri Lanka because they didn't want people to call it a hoax.

There were simultaneous bombings of three churches, a roof collapse in a church in South Africa where it crushed 13 people to death, and the burning cathedral.

Thirteen is the **number** of blood, fertility, and lunar potency. **13** is the lucky **number** of the Great **Goddess**. Representing as it does, the **number** of revolutions the moon makes around the earth in a year, **13** was the **number** of regeneration for pre-Columbian Mexicans. In ancient Israel, **13** was a sanctified **number**. Apr 13, 2012

The Goddess symbolism and the number 13 ties into Lauren London's debut on ATL on March 31,2006, which occurred 13 years to the date of Nipsey's death.

LIONS GATE AND NIPSEY RE-MEMBERED

Nipsey Hussle is a Leo. His birthday is on August 15th. In August they put a gate in front of The Marathon store. They closed it off.

themarathonclothing
The Marathon Store

· · ·

themarathonclothing #NipseyHussleTower

This would echo the celestial event called "The Lion's Gate" which occurs in August and pertains to the star Sirius, also known as a Phoenix to the occultists, as it passes the sign of Leo. This is all scripted according to the Astrotheological religion.

This gate was put up when they announced the construction of a Nipsey Hussle Memorial tower. They're putting a Memorial tower on the spot where he died.

Back to the Christ archetype: His death, and then the cathedral's tower falling symbolic of the sun god's castration to be followed by a "memorial tower" on the place of his death.

Putting his obelisk on his death site, which happens to be like Phoenix and like Dealey Plaza where Kennedy died happens to be on the 33rd parallel. This is all very ordered and structured. This is a very orderly rolled out a series of events.

It was published in a hot new hip hop.com that Nipsey Hustles', biographies going to be released and it's called "The Marathon Don't Stop".

All the different celebrations that go into this religion are based on the moon and the sun and the seasons and personification of the sun and the moon. It's on a calendar. And this is what gets me to say that these things are scripted. There is a Metascript. We're not looking at coincidences; we're looking at evidence of scripting.This thing is replete with symbolism and redundant symbolism like it's super obvious.

On Labor Day weekend, not only did you have a 33-year-old die at the burning man's 33rd festival, but 33 people burnt to death in a boat near Santa Barbara. And there was a bus with 33 kids in it that was involved in an accident that also made the news. So yes, there is a heavy amount of scripting here.

> 33 Man burning in front of white house predicted man dying at festival this summer, where a 33 year old dies, on the same weekend 33 burn to death in a boat fire, and 33 kids in a boat crash.

That's what it is. It's personified sun and his annual cycle is a lap on the marathon of life, death, and rebirth.

This story ties in a couple of things here: one, you have the space agencies; and two, you have the terrorist industry with the bombings in Sri Lanka and the insinuated involvement of ISIS in the Notre Dame fire.

They conflated that on purpose. The guy who saved the crown of thorns before it burned was a crisis actor with a record of involvement in the war on terror narrative. He was a hero at the Bataclan Eagles of Death Metal shooting and he was allegedly ambushed in Afghanistan.

And of course, ISIS bringing up and force-memeing the name ISIS into the public consciousness during Holy week.

A lot of it seems to be a form of typography, which is what Joseph Atwill describes when he talked about how the Roman Imperial cult inserted itself into the regional myths to make it seem divinely mandated to rule. Imposing myths on reality is what propaganda is all about. Religions are the original propagandists.

Jesus didn't make himself into a deity. His followers did. His apostles and the apostles of Nipsey Hussle are out there even today saying the marathon continues or the marathons continue forever and there they're still pushing it.

Recently, Snoop Dogg came out and he said if you're looking at Nipsey hustle's facial structure, you can see he's clearly Jesus Christ. Snoop even reference the age of 33. He suggested Nipsey's jawline makes him look like Jesus.

Finally, he said he's like Jesus in that few knew nipsey story in his lifetime.

It was after Christ died and people looked back and saw what he did that they wanted to be like him. And now one final note: Nipsey Hussle advanced the cashless society narrative when opened the world's first smart store.

This can be symbolically associated with the Mark of the Beast in a cashless society. So there's another layer of symbolism here. It's all very clever. It's very deep and very scripted. The story of Nipsey Hussle takes place within a scripted version of reality, the Metascript.

Who writes it you ask? The ones that write the bibles: Humanities rulers. The ones that control the media today.

PART 3

MANDOOZLED

The Mandela Effect Debunked

UNFALSIFIABLE

What can be asserted without evidence can also be
dismissed without evidence.
—Hitchens's Razor

Extraordinary claims without evidence can be
disregarded without reference to counter-evidence. The
claims of "the effected" are well intentioned
misrememberences and are unfalsifiable. They assert
their Mandela Effect is true even though the theory
cannot be contradicted by an observation or the
outcome of any physical experiment.

When one so called "Effect" is debunked, they move on
to the next one.

Nothing can prove it wrong. Just as nothing can prove
that aliens aren't abducting unicorns to vaccinate them

against chemtrails. The person making the claim owns the burden of proof. There is no obligation on behalf of the skeptic to provide evidence to counter such a claim. Occam's and Hitchen's Razors are enough.

THE MIRACLE EFFECT

Miracle: an extraordinary and astonishing happening that is attributed to the presence and action of an ultimate or divine power.

Why do people want the Mandela Effect to be true? Because it is miraculous. People choose to believe in miracles for many reasons. Its an escape from objective reality over which we are ostensibly powerless. Miracles make us players in a bigger, cosmic game.

Miracles are comforting, validating, and life-changing. The Mandela Effect, referred to as "ME" by its true believers, is a miraculous occurrence. To experience a Mandela Effect is to have penetrated the programming of the matrix and gleaned insights into the holographic, shifting, and subjective nature of reality.

Miracles have traditionally been associated with religions as their claims to authenticity. The performance of miracles in front of witnesses is all it takes to start a cult of believers.

Cults of believers provide all the social and cognitive reinforcement required to ensure the group grows. So long as the miracles are legitimate and the faith is strong, the cult will persist. Such aggregate of believers gain confidence and even belligerence as their numbers reinforce the meaningfulness of the miracle which brought them all together.

Leaders in such groups will invariably have to warn the believers about the non-believers, those heretics whose words have the power to disintegrate the cult. Such non-conformers must have to be corrected or exiled. These exiles will be demonized in the harshest of terms to ensure that the others don't make the same error.

WHAT CAUSES THE MANDELA EFFECT?

The Mandela Effect is caused by faulty eyewitness testimony influenced by the suggestions of the person who is pointing out the supposed discrepancy. Its not a paradigm-shattering revelation. It only appears that way to those who are affected.

A million people misremembering can add the illusion of credibility to any supposed Mandela Effect. It only takes a fraction of the population to mis-remember something for a viral video on the topic to get a show of support in favor of the supposed discrepancy.

"It has long been speculated that mistaken eyewitness identification plays a major role in the wrongful conviction of innocent individuals. A growing body of research now supports this speculation, indicating that mistaken eyewitness identification is responsible for more convictions of the innocent than all other factors combined.."   Source: https://en.wikipedia.org/wiki/Eyewitness_memory

"the Innocence Project determined that 75% of the 239 DNA exoneration cases had occurred due to inaccurate eyewitness testimony. It is important to inform the public about the flawed nature of eyewitness memory and the difficulties relating to its use in the criminal justice system so that eyewitness accounts are not viewed as the absolute truth."

The suggestion of a discrepancy is all it takes.

That suggestion of a misperception is an example of "gaslighting, a subtle form of psychological abuse where the victim is cause to doubt their own sanity and perception. When someone says "are you sure you know that?" it chips at your confidence in your own perceptions.

INTERROGATOR BIAS

The interrogator framing the question has great power to influence what is recollected. For example, if an interrogator asks, "notice anything strange about your favorite brand of peanut butter?" the answer would mostly be unrelated to the Mandela Effect.

But what if the question is posited as, "do you remember that famous brand of peanut butter as Jiff or Jiffy?", Then you have to choose your side---was it Jiffy or Jiff?

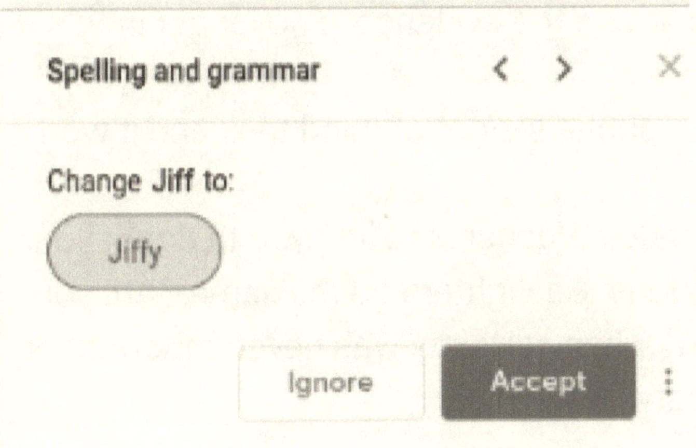

When such a question is asked, your cognitive bias towards what feels right will naturally lead to a confident response. That initial confidence plus the interrogator bias reinforces that answer.In the absense of counter evidence, they have no reason to doubt their recollection.

The problem is , there is no counter evidence. Either they remember it right and the evidence confirms this or they are wrong but their bias will now attach them to that wrong answers.

Bottom line: the Mandela Effected are wrong, but the way it was framed led them to choose the wrong answer where the evidence is no longer in this reality.

This is a subtle sleight of mind trick and it works.

The Mandela Pusher is telling you to doubt your perceptions. Gaslighters do the same. "Are you certain?" when certainty was never important or necessary.

It's not about Jiff or Jiffy or misremembered song lyrics. It has no implications for reality.

The gaslighting Mandela Effect Pusher get the questioner to accept the premise that reality is fake. Their job is to make reality a dream, simulation, or illusion, that way your critique of fake news carries no weight.

If you think the Earth is flat but you also think your dog was a cat yesterday, then you're no longer a credible witness of anything--and your a candidate for involuntary incarceration:

MISINFORMED CONSENSUS

"Witnesses can be subject to memory distortions that can alter their account of events. It is of particular interest that the memory of an eyewitness can become compromised by other information, such that an individual's memory becomes biased."

The Mandela Effected interrogator is contaminating the witnesses. This is called retroactive interference.

"Another phenomenon that may interfere with an eyewitness' memory is retroactive interference. This occurs when new information is processed that obstructs the retrieval of old information. A common source of interference that may occur after the event of a crime is the reporting of the crime. Police investigations include questioning that is often suggestive. The processing of new information may disrupt or entirely replace old information."

Source -
https://en.wikipedia.org/wiki/Ey
ewitness_memory

The matter is further complicated when large numbers of people who are in total agreement about something they are wrong about introduces social and cognitive reinforcements of those incorrect memories.

TO BELIEVE OR TO PERCEIVE

Psyops in the news are being exposed daily. Their way of contaminating the research pool is by suggesting people who don't believe or trust the news cannot trust their own perceptions nor trust their own judgment.

They use conspiracy theorists---people with theories and guesses but no real actionable evidence----to hide the real deceptions. The more they can get perceivers to doubt their perceptions, the more those perceivers will be forced to rely on experts.

The more they rely on experts, the less they know directly. This is what makes them into believers and followers.

THE MANDELA EFFECT AS SABOTAGE OPERATION AGAINST TRUTHERS

"NOTHING IS REAL EVERYTHING IS PERMITTED" -- Hassan-i Sabbah

President Trump said it may be necessary for people with mental illness to be 'involuntarily" confined. This was stated in the aftermath of the shooting at the Walmart in El Paso, TX.

Mandela Effect attacks the idea of objective reality.If nothing is objective, then there is no truth. A Mandela Effect affected person is in no position to take the media to task for making extraordinary statements without evidence. It's a self-discrediting for a perceiver to admit no ability to admit when they are caught in an emotional attachment to a wrong answer.

PART 4

WHY AUTOHOAXING MATTERS

SCHOOL SHOOTING DRILLS OR DOMESTIC TERRORISM?

Shooting drills are harmful to students, parents, and are damaging to society by polarizing people over political issues. The drills are potilical events with children being put in the middle of it as martyrs for the pro-gun control agena. This is a highly charged political issue and not a safety issue and the kids caught in the middle are being systematically terrorized. Drills cause PTSD and reinforce a worldview that is largely based on extreme-propaganda and not reality.

Hyper-Realistic shooting drills harmful in the following ways: chronic emotional distress is known to lead to complex and post-traumatic stress disorders and other delayed stress reactions. There are no long term research on the effects, but the causes of PTSD have been long understood.

Gun control advocates inflate the dangers of a statistical anomaly. They exaggerate the dangers. The news media sensationalizes a polarising topic and this gets surreptitiously inserted into the curriculum via shooter drills.

The intentional infliction of emotional duress is not education. It is a fear-based indoctrination. The harmful effects of this form of simulated violence are real.

In 2015 Linda McLean, an Elementary school teacher in Oregon sued for psychological harm. She was a victim of school shooting drill terrorism when a masked man in a hoodie walked into the classroom and shot her in the face with a blank. She was unaware of the drill and was predictably shocked.

Given the nature of these surprise attacks, she had no way to prepare for the shock. It must be pointed out that no one should ever have to stare down the barrel of a gun. This has no training value and represents a clear and present danger, as there can be accidental discharge or mistakes when sorting ammunition. Such errors can result in death and injuries.

The shooting scenarios used to terrify the students reinforce ideological biases and bigotries. For example, it is taught, in these drills, that white kids are the threat, and Second Amendment supporters are violent extremists and to be considered potential terrorists. Drill scenarios never scapegoat any other demographics. This is bigoted racially and politically.

Active shooter drills are predicated on the exaggerated threats

The U.S. Education Department reported that in the 2015-2016 school year nearly 240 schools had experienced school shooting incidents. Fact-checking by NPR revealed that only 11 of these were incidents, none of which had anything to do with actual gnu violence.

Young children experience simulated terror as a real terror. There's no training value in stimulating a real fight or flight response. This is Trauma Bonding students to the police armed with the very guns the students are trained to fear. Trauma Bonding also is known as Stockholm Syndrome, appears to be the real purpose of hyper-real shooting drills.

The intentional infliction of emotional duress for political purposes is terrorism by definition. The hyper-realistic drills are as gruesome as anything in an R-rated movie can present. Yet, they are used to scare children for reasons other than their safety. It appears to be an indoctrination mechanism of the state.

Teachers, Parents, Police are complicit in a domestic terror operation. These are not safety drills. The public schools are using terrorism to change minds and to

influence populations into giving up their rights.

NOTE FROM THE AUTHOR

Thanks to all of you who made it possible for me to have the time to get my thoughts out on paper. Read my blog at http://timozman.space or join the IPS http://infiniteplanesociety.com to stay in touch.

Tim Ozman

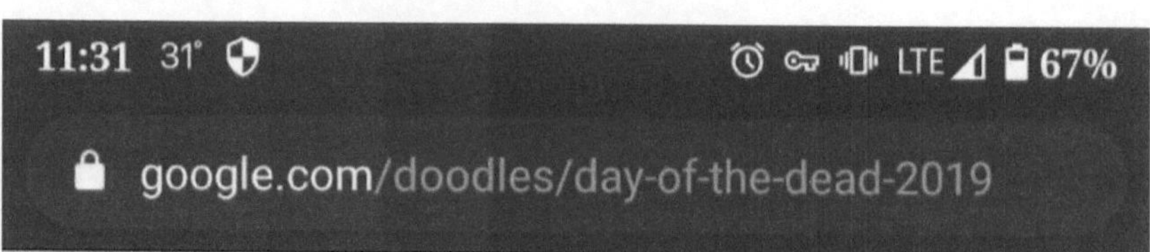

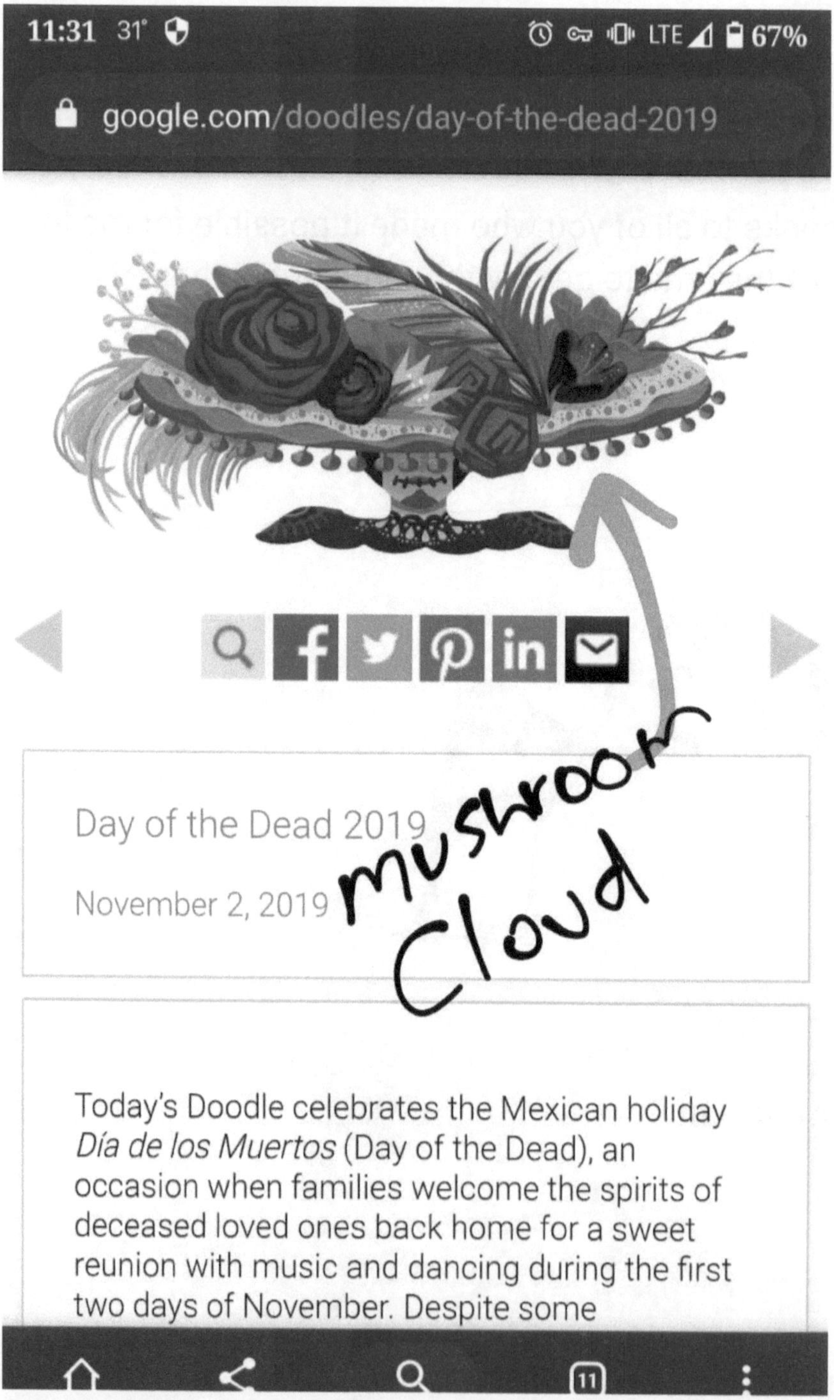
11:31 31° 67%
google.com/doodles/day-of-the-dead-2019
mushroom Cloud
Day of the Dead 2019
November 2, 2019
Today's Doodle celebrates the Mexican holiday *Día de los Muertos* (Day of the Dead), an occasion when families welcome the spirits of deceased loved ones back home for a sweet reunion with music and dancing during the first two days of November. Despite some
11

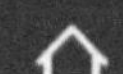

\#nofloorsmatter

www.ingramcontent.com/pod-product-compliance
Lightning Source LLC
Chambersburg PA
CBHW051459250726
48655CB00001B/493